Jeff Shavitz on

Small Business AhaMessages

140 Key Axioms That Every Business Owner Should Consider

By Jeff Shavitz

THiNKaha®
An Actionable Business Journal

E-mail: info@thinkaha.com
20660 Stevens Creek Blvd., Suite 210
Cupertino, CA 95014

Published by THiNKaha®
20660 Stevens Creek Blvd., Suite 210, Cupertino, CA 95014
http://thinkaha.com
E-mail: **info@thinkaha.com**

First Printing: October 2015
Paperback ISBN: 978-1-61699-158-6 (1-61699-158-5)
eBook ISBN: 978-1-61699-159-3 (1-61699-159-3)
Place of Publication: Silicon Valley, California, USA
Paperback Library of Congress Number: 2015947962

Trademarks

All terms mentioned in this book that are known to be trademarks or service marks have been appropriately capitalized. Neither THiNKaha, nor any of its imprints, can attest to the accuracy of this information. Use of a term in this book should not be regarded as affecting the validity of any trademark or service mark.

Warning and Disclaimer

Every effort has been made to make this book as complete and as accurate as possible. The information provided is on an "as is" basis. The author(s), publisher, and their agents assume no responsibility for errors or omissions. Nor do they assume liability or responsibility to any person or entity with respect to any loss or damages arising from the use of information contained herein.

How to Read a THiNKaha® Book
A Note from the Publisher

The THiNKaha series is the CliffsNotes of the 21st century. The value of these books is that they are contextual in nature. Although the actual words won't change, their meaning will change every time you read one as your context will change. Experience your own "aha!" moments ("AhaMessages™") with a THiNKaha book; AhaMessages are looked at as "actionable" moments—think of a specific project you're working on, an event, a sales deal, a personal issue, etc. and see how the AhaMessages in this book can inspire your own AhaMessages, something that you can specifically act on. Here's how to read one of these books and have it work for you.

1. Read a THiNKaha book (these slim and handy books should only take about 15–20 minutes of your time!) and write down one to three actionable items you thought of while reading it. Each journal-style THiNKaha book is equipped with space for you to write down your notes and thoughts underneath each AhaMessage.

2. Mark your calendar to re-read this book again in 30 days.

3. Repeat step #1 and write down one to three more AhaMessages that grab you this time. I guarantee that they will be different than the first time. BTW: this is also a great time to reflect on the actions taken from the last set of AhaMessages you wrote down.

After reading a THiNKaha book, writing down your AhaMessages, re-reading it, and writing down more AhaMessages, you'll begin to see how these books contextually apply to you. THiNKaha books advocate for continuous, lifelong learning. They will help you transform your ahas into actionable items with tangible results until you no longer have to say "aha!" to these moments—they'll become part of your daily practice as you continue to grow and learn.

As Chief Aha Instigator & CEO of THiNKaha, I definitely practice what I preach. I read *Alexisms and Ted Rubin on How to Look People in the Eye Digitally*, and one new book once a month and take away two to three different action items from each of them every time. Please e-mail me your ahas today!

Mitchell Levy
publisher@thinkaha.com

THiNKaha ®

Dedication

Dedicated to all the men and women who control their destiny in business success.

This book is also lovingly dedicated to my family - Jill, Jennifer, Lexi, and Andrew - who all mean the world to me.

Acknowledgement

According to different studies, there are approximately 15 million to 20 million small businesses in the United States. This book is dedicated to all the men and women who have pursued this career path. Congratulations!

Contents

Section 1

Why Make That Leap of Faith?

In this section, you'll find answers to the question that's been nagging you: Why should you leave your job and become an entrepreneur? Jeff presents a few convincing arguments about making that decision to change your life forever.

1

Starting your own business is hard, but it's also hard working as an employee for a company. Do it for yourself. @JeffShavitz

---

2

Do you have the traits to really be an "entrepreneur"? @JeffShavitz

---

3

Did you ever have a business "aha moment"? Act on it. @JeffShavitz

_____

_____

_____

4

Do you want to start a company?
Buy a company? Join a company?
Find the answer first, and then pursue it.
@JeffShavitz

_____

_____

_____

5

You're simply not the master of your life
when working for corporate America, and
the ultimate payoff is out of your control.
@JeffShavitz

_____

_____

_____

6

Why do otherwise sane men and women ever take up the life of the entrepreneur? Ask yourself why. @JeffShavitz

_____

_____

_____

7

Be truthful to who you are. Find your business passion to pursue! @JeffShavitz

_____

_____

_____

8

Never let money be the obstacle for starting a new business. A good idea will find capital for its growth. @JeffShavitz

_____

_____

_____

9

Do you love or like what you do?
Most people don't love it - but you can
be one of the few who do if
you plan accordingly.
@JeffShavitz

_____

_____

_____

10

Running a small business is quite different than working for a large corporation. @JeffShavitz

_____

_____

_____

11

Try something completely different and wacky this year for your business. @JeffShavitz

_____

_____

_____

12

Think about what "money" really means to you. It's a personal answer. @JeffShavitz

_____

_____

_____

13

We always hear 50% of start-up companies fail within a few years. Be optimistic, as you should be one of the 50% that succeed. @JeffShavitz

_____

_____

_____

14

Business ADD: Business Attention Deficit Disorder - I have it, do you? Focus each day on your priorities. @JeffShavitz

_____

_____

_____

15

Small business is a critical part of the world's economy. We are very important, and we can't forget that. @JeffShavitz

_____

_____

_____

16

Does each year go by where you want to leave "Corporate America" and become an entrepreneur and your own person? @JeffShavitz

_____

_____

_____

17

When was the last time you had a great idea
- but were lazy and did nothing about it?
@JeffShavitz

_____

_____

_____

18

Ideas are relatively easy to think of - it's the
execution that's hard. @JeffShavitz

_____

_____

_____

19

If you own a small business, you can give yourself any title you like & pick the corner office (even if it's in the basement)! @JeffShavitz

_____

_____

_____

20

Many brandnames become ubiquitous
overnight. In reality, they spent years
creating brand awareness & gaining
market acceptance. @JeffShavitz

_____

_____

_____

21

More than 600,000 of small businesses in the USA are franchisees. Great industry to explore if you haven't already. @JeffShavitz

_____

_____

_____

22

While Corporate America has been downsizing, the number of small business start-ups has grown and continues to grow rapidly. @JeffShavitz

_____

_____

_____

23

SBA reports that since 1990, statistics show that big business eliminated 4MM jobs while small companies created 8MM new jobs. @JeffShavitz

_____

_____

_____

24

There are approximately 20MM small businesses in the US & Small Business Administration accounts for 54% of all sales. @JeffShavitz

_____

_____

_____

Section II

How to Find Success in Small Business

After taking that leap, where to next? Here, you'll
learn good practices to follow and mistakes to
avoid to find success in your small
business venture.

25

When you have your own business,
when its good, it's great, and when it's bad,
it really sucks! @JeffShavitz

_____

_____

_____

26

Empathy is a very powerful word. Learn
from others, and respect all businesspeople,
as making money is hard. @JeffShavitz

_____

_____

_____

27

It's a trite expression to "learn from your failures." But it's true - if you don't learn, it really was a failure. @JeffShavitz

_____

_____

_____

28

What drives you for success? Is it only money? Be introspective and really understand your answer. @JeffShavitz

_____

_____

_____

29

Know your numbers: Successful business people know every month how their company is doing (and it's not just a gut feeling). @JeffShavitz

_____

_____

_____

30

Be patient - creating a successful company
rarely happens overnight. Never is probably
a better word to use. @JeffShavitz

_____

_____

_____

31

Is your goal to amass lots of small
accounts or a few big ones?
I think you know the answer. @JeffShavitz

_____

_____

_____

32

Do you have a business mentor to bounce ideas off of? Or a board of directors to get feedback on the sanity of your concepts? @JeffShavitz

_____

_____

_____

33

Big data is not just for Fortune
500 companies any longer. Analytics,
metrics & buying patterns are critical to
your success. @JeffShavitz

_____

_____

_____

34

Facts and numbers don't lie -
you can't make it up. @JeffShavitz

_____

_____

_____

35

Why do you work so hard? There must
be a reason. For me, it's "freedom."
What's your answer? @JeffShavitz

_____

_____

_____

36

Do your customers and employees really know what you are thinking? If not, share with them. @JeffShavitz

_____

_____

_____

37

When was the last time you invited a junior level person of your company out for lunch just to listen to their ideas? @JeffShavitz

_____

_____

_____

Section III

Today's Tricks of the Trade

In today's world, why is it that size doesn't matter? In this section, you'll be updated on the top trends in small business and the practical ways to win advocates and rake in revenues.

38

Read my book, "Size Doesn't Matter."
Great info for the small to mid-size
business owner. @JeffShavitz

_____

_____

_____

39

Pick up the phone, and call a minimum of
three existing customers to thank them for
their business and check in to say hello.
@JeffShavitz

_____

_____

_____

40

Have you already "made your decision"
before asking your team for their input?
@JeffShavitz

_____

_____

_____

41

Nothing happens without sales. Don't forget
those four simple words. @JeffShavitz

_____

_____

_____

42

No need to always invent a brand new product or service. Better yet, just improve on something already in the marketplace. @JeffShavitz

_____

_____

_____

43

Customers would rather buy a good
product from an extraordinary company
than an extraordinary product from
a bad company. @JeffShavitz

_____

_____

_____

44

When was the last time you "wasted" some money on a new business marketing project? I call it "investing." @JeffShavitz

_____

_____

_____

45

As a business owner, do you understand your credit card fees? There are lots of "hidden fees" to understand. @JeffShavitz

_____

_____

_____

46

Do you belong to a business group
and meet on a monthly business to
network and learn? @JeffShavitz

_____

_____

_____

47

Rising through corporate bureaucracy
from Analyst, Associate, VP, Senior VP
& President is no longer in vogue to
millenials. @JeffShavitz

_____

_____

_____

48

Heard of "residual income"? Is your org model transaction income or residual? It makes a difference to generating wealth.
@JeffShavitz

49

How many trade-shows and/or conventions do you attend each year? Make it more than four - get out and meet some new people.
@JeffShavitz

50

When did you last quantify the results of your last marketing campaign? Was it a gut reaction that "worked" or "didn't work"? @JeffShavitz

_____

_____

_____

51

Networking & Networking: Most people do it all wrong. Study your "ROT" (Return on Time) vs. your ROI (Return on Investment). @JeffShavitz

_____

_____

_____

52

Do you have the right people in your org?
Tell yourself the truth: Should you fire
somebody that doesn't fit your culture?
@JeffShavitz

_____

_____

_____

53

Think about it: Do your children who are
graduating from college now want to work
for companies like Xerox, IBM, or GE?
@JeffShavitz

_____

_____

_____

54

Pick up the phone every day, and call a minimum of three prospects to introduce yourself and your company. It's nice to hear from the CEO. @JeffShavitz

_____

_____

_____

55

Whatever money (or to sound business-like, "capital") you think you need for your business launch, double it! @JeffShavitz

_____

_____

_____

56

It's a good idea to listen to audio business books or podcasts when driving. Stop listening to satellite radio! @JeffShavitz

_____

_____

_____

57

Become friends with your competition.
It's a big world out there, so don't be scared
to share info with fellow competitors.
@JeffShavitz

_____

_____

_____

58

Start writing a blog - even if nobody reads it,
you can say that you are a blog author!
@JeffShavitz

_____

_____

_____

59

My favorite business quote: "The harder you work, the luckier you become." I think it's true. @JeffShavitz

_____

_____

_____

60

Are you aggravated when your corporate friends argue that they're entrepreneurs, though they've never paid for the FedEx bill? @JeffShavitz

_____

_____

_____

61

Network with people "NOT" like yourself.
It's too easy to always surround yourself
with people who share similar backgrounds.
@JeffShavitz

_____

_____

_____

62

When was the last time your company
was sued? If never, you're lucky,
but it's unfortunately coming.
Be prepared. @JeffShavitz

_____

_____

_____

63

Think about your disaster recovery plan. It's better to be prepared. Most business owners don't have one. @JeffShavitz

_____

_____

_____

64

Learn to play golf - it changed my business life. If not golf, find another sport to socialize with others. @JeffShavitz

_____

_____

_____

Section IV

Why Time Is Gold

This section is dedicated to those who seem to be always running out of time. It teaches us how to make the best out of time, with useful tips about planning your work and keeping in control.

65

As Benjamin Franklin stated in 1748, "Time is money." For the entrepreneur and small business owner, it definitely is! @JeffShavitz

_____

_____

_____

66

Monthly planning: Do you honestly know
if your company made or lost money last
month? Last week? Study the numbers.
@JeffShavitz

_____

_____

_____

67

Don't leave work until you have written down your plan and to-do list for the following day. @JeffShavitz

_____

_____

_____

68

When was the last time you reviewed your 1-year, 3-year, or 5-year plan? Do you even have a plan for next month? @JeffShavitz

_____

_____

_____

69

Work an extra hour per day. Assuming
270 work days per year, that equals
270 hours, which is another
39 work days in a year. @JeffShavitz

70

Is it time to sell your business and become
an employee again? @JeffShavitz

Section V

Work/Life Balance

Work never stops. How do you keep yourself from burning out? In this section, you will know why it's good to set up a no-work zone at home.

71

Do you have a passion and/or hobby outside of work that you are really committed to? If not, find one. @JeffShavitz

_____

_____

_____

72

Are you happy with the combination of your business and personal life? Just give a "yes" or "no" answer. @JeffShavitz

_____

_____

_____

73

How many hours do you work a day as a
business owner? It never stops, right?
@JeffShavitz

_____

_____

_____

74

Establish a "no work zone" in your home - don't always talk shop with your partner or significant other, it gets boring. @JeffShavitz

_____

_____

_____

75

Do you really "love" what you do for a living? I like it a lot. but I would rather be with my family or playing golf. @JeffShavitz

_____

_____

_____

76

Teach your children the value of money.
@JeffShavitz

_____

_____

_____

77

Why did I "lie" to my employees when I
was leaving work early to play golf? I don't
know. It's my company & my risk. Guilt?
@JeffShavitz

_____

_____

_____

78

Surprise your SO and/or children - take the day off for no reason to spend quality time with them. The office will be fine.
@JeffShavitz

_____

_____

_____

79

Don't check your cellphone in the middle of the night, even if an idea pops into your brain. Write it down & go back to sleep.
@JeffShavitz

_____

_____

_____

80

Are you genuinely happy for your best friend who married into a successful family business? Be honest! @JeffShavitz

_____

_____

_____

81

The saga of the family business: Is it for you to join your mom/dad or brother/sister or relative? @JeffShavitz

_____

_____

_____

82

Don't text and drive. Your company can wait
for the response. Be a responsible human
being. @JeffShavitz

_____

_____

_____

Section VI

Notes to Self as the Business Owner

In this section, Jeff talks to the owner of the small business – you. How do you practice leadership? What are the things you want to achieve, and who will work for you to achieve it?

83

Close your eyes, and take three slow breaths at work today and every day. It will make for a more effective workday! @JeffShavitz

_____

_____

_____

84

Know what you are good at - is it working with #s, people, or strategies? Understand yourself and how you can best contribute. @JeffShavitz

_____

_____

_____

85

Negotiate a fair deal. Put yourself in the other party's position. @JeffShavitz

_____

_____

_____

86

Amazing how many people will not do proper prospect follow-up and lose the sale. Are you one of them? @JeffShavitz

_____

_____

_____

87

Most people are jealous of your success. Only ask people for advice who you truly trust and respect. @JeffShavitz

_____

_____

_____

88

Think whether you want to create an org
of a handful of employees or to work alone.
There is no right answer to the question.
@JeffShavitz

_____

_____

_____

89

Have you already thought of your "exit" before starting the company? Enjoy the journey first, and the exit will come. @JeffShavitz

_____

_____

_____

90

Welcome to the Entrepreneurs' Club - wouldn't you agree that there is an immediate bond when you meet a fellow entrepreneur? @JeffShavitz

_____

_____

_____

91

Don't just start an org because you love
your hobby. With this logic, every college
jock would start a sports memorabilia shop.
@JeffShavitz

92

Helping with non-profits and other
philanthropic causes will make you a better
human being and a better businessperson.
@JeffShavitz

93

We all have different priorities and your values matter - never deviate from your personal mission with your company. @JeffShavitz

_____

_____

_____

94

What is your personality trait? Type A?
Good guess. @JeffShavitz

_____

_____

_____

95

Do the business tasks that you hate doing first thing in the morning. By 10:30AM, you should be done with this work. @JeffShavitz

_____

_____

_____

96

Do your corporate friends ever go to bed wondering about making payroll? Probably not. Jealous? Don't be an entrepreneur. @JeffShavitz

_____

_____

_____

97

As a business owner, I hate the annual holiday review period for employee raises and bonuses. The employee now expects it.
@JeffShavitz

_____

_____

_____

98

Surround yourself with a management team that has different skill sets than yourself. @JeffShavitz

_____

_____

_____

99

Corporate America has meetings to have more meetings. @JeffShavitz

_____

_____

_____

100

The best way to sell and open a new business account is to pick up the phone and call. It's pretty simple. @JeffShavitz

_____

_____

_____

101

Decisions, decisions, and more decisions -
as a business owner, you better be prepared
to make them and make them quickly.
@JeffShavitz

_____

_____

_____

102

For the "older" generation, learn about
social media and how to use it.
Have you heard of Facebook and Twitter?
@JeffShavitz

_____

_____

_____

103

There is a difference between "employer" and "employee" - they're both people with different perspectives. Understand each other. @JeffShavitz

_____

_____

_____

104

When you interview employees, do you have a key question you always ask? And will that answer determine whether you hire them? @JeffShavitz

_____

_____

_____

105

Branding is very different than marketing - make sure that you understand the difference. @JeffShavitz

_____

_____

_____

106

When was the last time that you updated your website? If over 6 months, it probably needs a refresh. @JeffShavitz

_____

_____

_____

107

Forget the three-year plan - write down three things you want to accomplish this month. And then do them. @JeffShavitz

_____

_____

_____

108

Don't even think about becoming the office psychologist, it can only backfire. @JeffShavitz

_____

_____

_____

109

If a specific employee is always calling in sick on Mondays and Fridays, are they really sick? Think about it. @JeffShavitz

_____

_____

_____

110

As you walk down your office hallway, check if you see people's computer screens quickly switching from Facebook to their work. @JeffShavitz

_____

_____

_____

111

How can your employee ALWAYS finish their job at 5PM? They start cleaning up at 4:45 to get ready to leave. @JeffShavitz

_____

_____

_____

112

Hire slowly, and fire quickly - Best advice I ever learned from a human resources perspective. @JeffShavitz

_____

_____

_____

113

Don't give out golf bags if you host a golf
tournament. Everyone already has one.
How else would they carry their clubs?
@JeffShavitz

_____

_____

_____

114

Don't send overnight shipping unless you really have to - if it's so important for the client, then let them pay for it! @JeffShavitz

_____

_____

_____

115

Backup all your important passwords and computer logins. For $.99, you can use an iPhone application. Good investment! @JeffShavitz

_____

_____

_____

116

If you have a superstar employee in your company, do you show them favoritism? @JeffShavitz

_____

_____

_____

117

Yoga, although I'm terrible at it, has become an enjoyable hour for me. @JeffShavitz

_____

_____

_____

118

Do your due diligence before hiring
someone. Of course their references
will be good. Dig deeper. @JeffShavitz

_____

_____

_____

119

Show your appreciation & write thank you notes. The handwritten note is a lost art - pick up a pen & paper & send it US Mail.
@JeffShavitz

_____

_____

_____

120

Get involved in a cause - just do something (and money is the easy way out). Dedicate time and money to help others.
@JeffShavitz

_____

_____

_____

121

Similar to leaving at 5PM, it's funny to watch some employees always get to the office exactly at 9AM! @JeffShavitz

_____

_____

_____

122

Many people have different aspirations,
interests & skill sets. This is good,
or everyone would want to be the boss.
@JeffShavitz

_____

_____

_____

123

Customers have a hard time finding great
vendors. Don't sell yourself short and
charge a competitive price. @JeffShavitz

_____

_____

_____

124

Is your business idea really that original? Probably not - it's the execution that will make the difference. @JeffShavitz

_____

_____

_____

125

A commodity can always be sold at a lower price. You are not a commodity. @JeffShavitz

_____

_____

_____

126

Spend money on joining business groups. Young Presidents Organization, Strategic Forum & Vistage have been invaluable to me. @JeffShavitz

_____

_____

_____

127

I put my bookkeeper in jail - not kidding!
Hire the right people. @JeffShavitz

_____

_____

_____

128

Review monthly bank & credit card
statements. Whether or not you have a CFO,
you need to understand your cash flow.
@JeffShavitz

_____

_____

_____

129

Have you completed your business and vision statement? Is it all fluff? Or does it mean something special for your company?
@JeffShavitz

_____

_____

_____

130

"Building relationships" - that's what I tell my employees when I want to go golfing for the afternoon. @JeffShavitz

_____

_____

_____

131

Read a business book this week - if not the
whole book, then at least the back cover to
learn something new! @JeffShavitz

_____

_____

_____

132

Death by over-planning - at some point, just
get out there and start. @JeffShavitz

_____

_____

_____

133

Don't forget to add the "waste money expense line item" into your budget. With this money, try cool stuff to promote growth. @JeffShavitz

_____

_____

_____

134

Make yourself feel vulnerable and get out of your comfort zone. You'll feel alive, and your company will thrive. @JeffShavitz

_____

_____

_____

135

Do the things you hate doing first thing in the morning to get them over with! @JeffShavitz

_____

_____

_____

136

If you are doing administrative tasks not par with "your greatest value," hire an assistant to do it for you. Time is money. @JeffShavitz

_____

_____

_____

137

The Law of Reciprocity always works in business. If you help someone, it does come back to you in a positive way. It works! @JeffShavitz

---

138

There is an expression, "Don't judge a book by its cover." I disagree; a first impression is an everlasting impression. @JeffShavitz

---

139

Invest money and time into your employees. Company morale amongst your team is critical to success. @JeffShavitz

_____

_____

_____

140

Many business owners need to work "on" their business vs. "in" their business.
@JeffShavitz

_____

_____

_____

What Are Your Ahas?

Thanks for reading *Jeff Shavitz on Small Business AhaMessages*!

Got any "AhaMessages" that would fit with this book?

We'd love for you to share them!

Tweet us **@happyabout** and/or **@JeffShavitz**, and tag it with **#smallbiz**.

About the Author

Jeff Shavitz is a successful entrepreneur. He worked as an investment banker at Lehman Brothers in the Corporate Finance/Mergers and Acquisitions Group, specializing in transactions ranging from $250MM–$500MM. With an offer in hand to attend graduate school to earn his MBA and continue his climb up the corporate ladder, Jeff consciously decided to leave this fast-paced, well-paying position to start up a one-person business. Friends said, "What is he thinking?"

A passion for creating "a life of his own" was the driving force in determining Jeff's business future. Out of his New York apartment, while still working on Wall Street, he created "Spectoculars," a branded paper-folding binocular that received an NFL license in 1991. At Super Bowl XXX, 250,000 pairs were distributed.

Fast-forward several years and Jeff cofounded Charge Card Systems Inc., a national credit card processing company that helps merchants with their processing requirements, including the acceptance of Visa, MasterCard, American Express, and Discover. The company grew to more than 700 sales agents throughout the country with three regional offices. In 2012, Jeff and his partners sold the business to Card Connect, owned by private equity firm FTV Capital. The purchase was the company's largest acquisition to date.

The culmination of Jeff's past experiences with the small and mid-size business owners is TrafficJamming LLC (www.trafficjamming.com), a membership association for business owners and entrepreneurs. All businesses want more traffic—in essence, traffic means sales. TrafficJamming provides its members with a destination website filled with information, technology tools, and insights to help grow your business. TrafficJamming is not a buying club or traditional business group, but rather, a modern organization to help executives realize their professional dreams. Among its many services, TrafficJamming provides proven and cutting-edge technology solutions to help build awareness of our members' products and services—with the ultimate goal of building a loyal tribe of clients.

In addition to *Jeff Shavitz on Small Business AhaMessages*™, Jeff has also published the following books:

– *Size Doesn't Matter*, which hit #1 on the Amazon new releases in Entrepreneurship. In this book, Jeff details his personal and professional experiences, observations, challenges, and rewards in operating small businesses.

– *Jeff Shavitz on The Power of Residual Income*, a collection of 140 AhaMessages which educates business owners on the power of residual and recurring income versus transactional income; and,

– *Jeff Shavitz on Networking*, a collection of 140 AhaMessages that discusses the most effective ways to nurture business relationships. Jeff has developed a philosophy that networking involves "Return on Time" (ROT) — using time properly to develop trusted and authentic relationships to help grow your company.

Jeff received his Bachelor of Arts degree in Economics from Tufts University and spent one semester at the London School of Economics, specializing in finance. He is very active in numerous charitable and civic community organizations and business groups, including Young Presidents' Organization.

He is married and has two daughters, a son, and two dogs. Besides being with family, enjoying good health, and living to see worldwide peace, Jeff's selfish goal is to play the 100 top golf courses in the United States.

To learn more about the author, visit www.JeffShavitz.com or contact him at jeff@trafficjamming.com or 800-878-4100.

Aha

A m p l i f i e r™
Democratizing Thought Leadership

The Aha Amplifier™ is the only thought leadership platform with a built in marketplace making it easy to share curated content from like-minded thought leaders. There are over 25k diverse AhaMessages™ from thought leaders from around the world.

The Aha Amplifier makes it easy to create, organize and share your own thought leadership AhaMessages in digestible, bite-sized morsels. Users are able to democratize thought leadership in their organizations by: 1) Making it easy for any advocate to share existing content with their Twitter, Facebook, LinkedIn & Google+ networks. 2) Allowing internal experts to create their own thought leadership content, and 3) Encouraging the expert's advocates to share that content on their networks.

The experience of many authors is that they have been able to create their social media enabled AhaBooks™ of 140 AhaMessages in less than a day.

Sign up for a free account at
http://www.AhaAmplifier.com today!

Please pick up a copy of this book in the Aha Amplifier
and share each AhaMessage socially at
http://aha.pub/smallbiz.